52

TUESDAYS

with

SAM CHAND

POWERFUL INSIGHTS TO INSPIRE
YOUR LEADERSHIP JOURNEY

S
M
T
W
T
F
S

52 Tuesdays With Sam Chand: Powerful Insights to Inspire Your Leadership Journey

by Sam Chand

copyright ©2019
ISBN: 978-1-950718-21-4
Printed in the United States of America

cover design by Joe DeLeon

CONTENTS

PART IV: CULTURE

INTRODUCTION

TUESDAYS WITH SAM CHAND is a weekly video series I designed to help encourage and inspire leaders and teams. For years, I've been sharing short messages with fellow leaders in both business and ministry circles. The feedback we've received from leaders and teams around the globe has been astounding! From those who watch TWSC videos in their staff meetings, to personal encounters with people whose perspectives have been shifted, seeing the positive impact of TWSC has brought us great joy.

Because these truths and reminders have been so effective for so many, it's our desire to compile a year's worth of TWSC content—the best of the best. That's why we created *52 Tuesdays with Sam Chand*. While you may absolutely read at your own pace, there is one message for every week of the year, to keep you motivated and inspired to chase your vision. At the end of each entry is a takeaway question that will help you consider how to practically apply the truths we've discussed.

Whatever dream you have—whatever calling God has given you—it requires that you constantly grow and develop into more than you have ever been. My heart is to help you succeed, and I sincerely believe this collection will help you do just that.

In addition, this is a great resource to share with your friends who are leaders, with your executive team, or with your employees. Our prayer is that it brings you together with the supportive people around you and makes your entire organization healthier, more successful, and more fulfilled.

Thank you for spending so many Tuesdays with me. Here's to many, many more.

—*Sam Chand*

PART I:
CHARACTER

day 1

BE MARY AND MARTHA!

MOST OF US know the story from Luke 10 about Mary and Martha: The women have a house full of guests, including Jesus. Martha is serving people, preparing food and making sure everyone is taken care of, while Mary is sitting at the feet of Jesus.

Over the years, many people have thrown Martha under the bus for being busy, and have elevated Mary for sitting still. Jesus never said, however, that we had to choose to be one or the other. He said, "*If* you have to make a choice, Mary's way would be better." But I'm here to share some good news with you—we don't have to make a choice! We can be Mary and Martha on a daily basis!

In your organization, you want people who are both spiritual and serving, right? You want people who are both worshipping and working. Wouldn't it be wonderful if your assimilation plan incorporated raising people up in both of these areas? We can train others to serve the Lord with gladness, and to worship Him at the same time! This is spirituality and service combined well.

IN YOUR ORGANIZATION, YOU WANT PEOPLE WHO ARE BOTH SPIRITUAL AND SERVING.

So when you have people in your organization—especially if your organization is a church—who are only serving, ask them how are they doing spiritually. There are some people who are doing well spiritually: how are they serving? Because serving people need spirituality, and spiritual people need to serve. We each need to be both Mary and Martha.

TAKEAWAY

Are you more of a Mary or a Martha? How can you cultivate the opposite characteristic in your daily walk with God?

_____

_____

_____

_____

_____

_____

_____

_____

_____

_____

_____

_____

_____

_____

_____

_____

_____

_____

_____

_____

LEARN, UNLEARN, RELEARN

A LVIN TOFFLER SAID, "The illiterate of the future will not be people who cannot read or write; but the illiterate of the future will be people who cannot learn, unlearn, and relearn."

The question for us is this: what do we need to unlearn? Whether we're unlearning a certain way of thinking, a set of assumptions, or a certain method of doing things, it's always going to be harder than learning. Our brains are already programmed with so many ideas and so much information, that it takes a concentrated effort to rewire them. This effort is what too many leaders neglect to give; and for this reason, they're headed towards becoming illiterate.

The truth is that we cannot remain the same. Everybody's changing—including you! It may be time to retire an old way of doing things, in favor of a fresh perspective. With new seasons come new methods, strategies, and vision.

THE GREATEST BLOCKAGE TO YOUR SUCCESS IS PREVIOUS SUCCESS, BECAUSE PREVIOUS SUCCESS MAKES US THINK WE'VE GOT IT ALL TOGETHER.

For instance, some people complain, "These days, people just aren't committed anymore!" People are committed, but in a different way. For Baby Boomers, commitments were lifelong ones. Now, commitments are serial—short-term. So you see, we have to learn and study the times we're living in right now—not yesterday. Not last week.

What do you know that's getting in the way of what you need to know? What are you doing that's getting in the way of what you need to be doing? The greatest blockage to your success is previous success, because previous success makes us think we've got it all together. If you're willing to learn, unlearn, and relearn, your future is brilliant.

TAKEAWAY

What do you need to unlearn? What methods of thinking (or action) have you kept with you from a previous period of success? How could those methods be holding you back from future successes?

_____
_____
_____
_____
_____
_____
_____
_____
_____
_____
_____
_____
_____
_____
_____
_____
_____
_____

BECOMING A WORLD-CHANGER

A FEW YEARS AGO, on a trip I took, I remember standing in Nelson Mandela Square, in Johannesburg, South Africa. When we think of and remember Nelson Mandela today, we consider him a world-changer. The question that came to my mind as I stood looking at his statue was this: How do individuals like him become world-changers? How do they begin? Are they born with special pedigrees that qualify them to be world-changers? If so, most of us are out of luck.

I don't believe this is the case. World-changers are simply ordinary people doing extraordinary things.

How do they begin? They begin with an idea—a thought. These individuals think, "Wow. I see a need here. I'd like to make a difference.' World-changers begin to identify the needs of their community, and they go a step further—they meet those needs. They make a difference. One thing leads to another—years of work and legacy-building—and, eventually, they become world-changers.

WORLD-CHANGERS BEGIN TO IDENTIFY THE NEEDS OF THEIR COMMUNITY, AND THEY GO A STEP FURTHER—THEY MEET THOSE NEEDS.

Today, I want to encourage you. Perhaps you want to change the world in some way, but feel overwhelmed, or unsure how to begin. Be sure of this: it won't come about because of any strategic plan, conference, or seminar. It won't happen all at once—so don't put that pressure on yourself. Your world-changing journey will only start when you get passionate about the needs around you. Begin to make a difference where you are! Seek the Lord, and take one small step at a time.

Who knows? One day, there may even be a square named after you. Even if there isn't, you'll be making a lasting difference for those around you. And that's the true definition of a world-changer.

TAKEAWAY

What are the needs that you see in your community? How can you take steps to meet those needs? Take a few moments to prayerfully examine your motives. Are you satisfied with doing this for the Lord and for people around you, or is there something else you're seeking?

_____

_____

_____

_____

_____

_____

_____

_____

_____

_____

_____

_____

_____

_____

_____

_____

day 4

SOONER OR LATER

THINK ABOUT THE small businesses you see on a daily basis. They may be law firms, retail shops, pet-adoption agencies...the variety is nearly endless. Every organization begins with someone who works with their friends or family. The only people they have to support them are those who love them the most. Then, as the business grows, these friends become employees.

When this happens, a big change occurs. It's a change we often miss, and seldom talk about in our organizational circles. Any time someone else controls your work schedule and tells you what to do, you cannot maintain the same relationship you had before they signed your paycheck. Yes, as a leader, you can still honor and respect your employees; but the positions on the board have shifted.

The time we spend with family members who work for us outside of work will decrease. Friends have drifted apart because of work situations like this. There will inevitably be changes in your relationship. It's important to acknowledge and accept this *before* you hire a close friend or family member, so that both parties are prepared for it.

KEEP IN MIND THE CHASM BETWEEN "EMPLOYEE" AND "FRIEND." SOONER OR LATER, YOU'LL HAVE TO DEAL WITH IT.

Friends may drift apart after a time. Family may not always be able to talk about non-work subjects with the same ease. Even when you communicate on the front end of the change, friendship still has its limits. You must govern your employees with an employer mindset—not a friend mindset. It can be difficult to do, but the success of your organization depends on it.

Simply put, keep in mind the chasm between "employee" and "friend." Sooner or later, you'll have to deal with it.

TAKEAWAY

Have you ever worked with or for a family member? Have you ever had a family member or friend work for you? What did you observe about the different dynamics that happen when family members sign each other's paychecks?

_____

_____

_____

_____

_____

_____

_____

_____

_____

_____

_____

_____

_____

_____

_____

_____

_____

_____

day 5

WHY YOU SHOULD GET RE-CERTIFIED

N 2015, I MADE a visit to the Taj Mahal in India. It was a wonderful experience. Our tour guide took us around, showed us the sights, and told us all about the historicity of the place. I began talking to him, and we struck up a conversation. At one point, I asked, "So, what was the process for you to become a tour guide?"

He showed me his license and said, "Every three years, I have to go in for a re-certification." I thought, *Re-certification? The Taj Mahal was built in the 1600s! Nothing has changed about it, right?* I then asked the obvious follow-up: "What do you have to get re-certified for?"

His answer was simple: the re-certification wasn't about the site changing; it was about ensuring the on-going quality and skill of the tour guides representing it to people around the world. I then began thinking... many of us preach the gospel of Jesus Christ. Many others serve in corporate or executive settings. We have a specialty, a trade, a calling—and many elements of that calling never change. The gospel, certainly, never changes. So the question is this: what are *we* doing to get regularly "re-certified?"

HONESTLY EVALUATE YOUR CURRENT PERFORMANCE AND KNOWLEDGE. WOULD YOU HIRE YOURSELF AGAIN?

Ask yourself a few pointed questions today; honestly evaluate your current performance and knowledge. Would you hire yourself again? Would you re-certify yourself at the level you serve today? Think about what it would take to re-certify yourself this year. What can you grow in? How can you test yourself? Then, get to it!

TAKEAWAY

Would you hire yourself again? In your calling and/or position, what has changed in the last few years? How can you anticipate and prepare for future changes so that you continually "re-certify" yourself?

_____

_____

_____

_____

_____

_____

_____

_____

_____

_____

_____

_____

_____

_____

_____

day 6

GROWTH EQUALS PAIN

'VE DISCOVERED THE ONE differentiating factor between a high-level leader and someone who has plateaued. Do you want to know what it is? It's not experience, skill, money, or connections. It's not bravado or humility or even a collaborative spirit. What holds leaders back? This simple truth does: you will grow only to the threshold of your pain. The more pain you can handle, the higher you can go. Why is this?

Because growth equals change. Every time you grow, something in your life is changing. Change equals loss. You lose something in order to move forward—comfort, people, the status quo. Loss equals pain. We don't like to let go of things; it doesn't come naturally to us as humans.

And so, growth equals pain. We each have a pain capacity. If you heighten your capacity, you can also grow higher. They're directly proportional. If you are the primary leader in your organization, your pain threshold will either elevate you, stagnate you, or drag you down. It will do the same for your organization. If you want to predict how far a business or ministry will go, simply take a look at the pain threshold of the person at the top.

YOU WILL ONLY GROW TO THE THRESHOLD OF YOUR PAIN.

The truth is that no leadership role comes without pain. We don't like pain, and it can mess with our heads. However, we have the choice to understand, embrace, and push through this pain. Indeed, that is the mark of true leadership. The higher you go, the greater the pain will be. That is why you will only grow to the threshold of your pain. So...how much do you want to grow?

TAKEAWAY

How has pain kept you from moving forward as a leader? How can you work on increasing your pain threshold so that these challenges don't stunt your growth and advancement in the future?

_____

_____

_____

_____

_____

_____

_____

_____

_____

_____

_____

_____

_____

_____

_____

_____

_____

_____

day 7

HOW TO MAKE YOUR LEGACY LAST

N THE CITY OF Delhi, India, stands the majestic Qutub Minar, a tower that imitates the silhouette of the Leaning Tower of Pisa in Italy. This impressive structure was built by a king over 2,000 years ago. He chose to use an innovative design, selecting interlocking, quality materials instead of mortar or cement. The results stand strong to this day—a testament to the legacy of hard, quality work.

However, just to the side of the Qutub Minar sits a neighboring tower. This copycat was built by what we would consider a "competing" king. This second king craved the glory of constructing a tower like the Qutub

Minar but chose to employ cheap materials in his own tower. He wanted the fame, without putting in the years of hard work. Instead of interlocking, expensive materials, the copycat king used dirt and bricks. He tried to form a timeless tower out of standard stuff.

WHAT YOU PAY FOR IS WHAT WILL DEFINE YOUR LEGACY IN THE YEARS TO COME.

Today, what does his tower look like? It's half-built. It's not even an entire structure any longer. It sits, squat, in the shadow of the Qutub Minar. The lesson is clear: if you want your legacy to last, it's not only essential to clarify what you're building—you also must know what you're building *with*!

What materials are you using in your organization today? Are they quality ones? Or have you settled for cheap, quick fixes in an effort to expedite the process? What you pay for is what will define your legacy in the years to come. Simply put, use good stuff!

TAKEAWAY

Are you building with quality materials? How can you focus more on this in your current season? What difference do you believe that will make in your future?

_____

_____

_____

_____

_____

_____

_____

_____

_____

_____

_____

_____

_____

_____

_____

_____

_____

_____

_____

day 8

WHEN YOU MAKE MISTAKES

I F YOU'RE LIVING, breathing, and doing anything of value, you will make mistakes. It's simply a fact of life. The only people who don't make mistakes are dead people (and people who are not doing anything). If you assume you don't make mistakes, you've just made one! There are four crucial things we need to do, not if, but *when* we make mistakes.

The first thing is to catch ourselves. When you mess up, 'fess up. You may think nobody has noticed, and you may not get confronted about it, but people notice. If you don't catch yourself, you'll lose equity with your team.

Number two is to actually confess to the mistake. Whatever department you messed up in, bring it to other people's attention. Have a chat with your team, your boss, or your supervisor. Identify what you did wrong. This leads us to the third thing...

Learn. You must identify what you've learned from the mistake in order for it to be fruitful. Did you learn to ask for permission? To lighten up? To not do something ever again? Identify the lesson, and move forward with that understanding.

YOU MUST IDENTIFY WHAT YOU'VE LEARNED FROM THE MISTAKE IN ORDER FOR IT TO BE FRUITFUL.

Fourth, we have to make new mistakes. This goes against our natural grain. But if we're constantly afraid of making them, we'll never go higher—we'll create a ceiling for ourselves in terms of vision. Don't play it safe. Make new mistakes; just don't repeat the old ones. Making new mistakes says you are trying new things in new areas—and that is crucial for a leader.

Let's recap: catch yourself, confess, learn, and make new mistakes. When you put these four elements together, you can start to make mistakes in the healthiest, most productive way possible.

TAKEAWAY

When was the last time you made a big mistake? Which of the four steps did you successfully complete? What did you learn from this mistake, and how will that help you moving forward?

_____

_____

_____

_____

_____

_____

_____

_____

_____

_____

_____

_____

_____

_____

_____

_____

_____

_____

day 9

BE A TOUR GUIDE

H AVE YOU EVER gone on vacation, or a business trip, and enlisted the help of travel agents or tour guides? If so, you know that these two professionals have distinct abilities and specialized tasks in the travel process that make the experience much more enjoyable for visitors.

A travel agent gets you to where you want to go. It's possible they have never set foot in the location themselves; but they know how to get you there. They're experts when it comes to modes of transportation. After you've arrived, the travel agent has done his job, and he hands off the proverbial baton to a tour guide.

A tour guide, in contrast, knows the location intimately. He goes there every day. He's spent months studying about it, and talking about it. He understands the significance, the history, of that destination enough to answer any questions you can possibly ask.

DON'T SIMPLY SETTLE FOR BEING A TRAVEL AGENT AND GETTING PEOPLE IN THE FRONT DOOR. BE A TOUR GUIDE!

Do you know what would be great to implement in our organizations? An ethic that doesn't stop at simply sending or inviting people to our organization, but intentionally makes an effort to show them around once they get there. If you knew enough about your company—business, church, nonprofit—to take them on a detailed tour, don't you think that would help them see the significance? Wouldn't it be great to help others feel the history, the beauty, of your organization, and bring value to their lives?

Don't simply settle for being a travel agent, and getting people through the front door. Be a tour guide!

TAKEAWAY

What "travel agent" skills do you bring to the table in your organization? What "tour guide" skills do you practice? How can you focus on showing the value of your organization to others?

_____

_____

_____

_____

_____

_____

_____

_____

_____

_____

_____

_____

_____

_____

_____

_____

_____

day 10

WHAT'S YOUR HEART?

EVERY ORGANIZATION HAS a heart—including yours. We've all heard the term "assimilation" thrown around in business or ministry circles. That's because the heart of your organization is revealed by how you assimilate new members into it. Let's see how this plays out on a practical level.

If someone came to your church this weekend, accepted Christ, and became a member, what would your plan for that person's life be? How would you engage them at every level? What would the markers of "success" be for your church? How would you know you'd met your goals and their needs effectively? Most churches don't have a systematic process for each stage of a member's growth. Instead, they wait until the person has jumped through all the hoops to finally engage them fully. When we do this, we're revealing, at some level, the heart of our organization.

HOW YOU ONBOARD A PERSON WILL DEFINE THEIR LONGEVITY AND PRODUCTIVITY.

Here's an even more pertinent example: think about your assimilation process with new employees. If someone was to come to work for you today—and today was Day One—what would your plans be for that person's life? Do you have any? Will you simply begin where every organization begins—with HR, policies and procedures? Or, instead, will you teach this new team member about your culture, making sure they're a good fit before you do anything else? Will you invest in them and work to make them a better employee?

Most organizations—sacred and secular—haven't thought out this process. You can choose to keep winging it, if you like. However, this is what you need to know: it will cost you three times the amount of time, energy, and money to find a replacement after you fail to assimilate someone than it will to bring in someone the right way. How you onboard a person will define their longevity and productivity. Engage the person's heart, and they'll see your heart, as well.

TAKEAWAY

What is your assimilation process for new members? What about new employees? How can you fine-tune this process to include assimilation and personal development on every level of this person's journey with you?

_____

_____

_____

_____

_____

_____

_____

_____

_____

_____

_____

_____

_____

_____

_____

_____

_____

day 11

A DEADLY LOVE

ERHAPS YOU'VE HEARD the Greek legend of Narcissus, who saw his reflection in a pool, fell in love with himself, leaned closer and closer, fell into the water, and drowned. Narcissism, we see, is falling in love with yourself. Unfortunately, this disease is rampant in our society. An even greater misfortune is that it often percolates underneath the surface, disguised as self-effacing humility. These unchecked pockets of narcissism are especially prevalent in leadership.

Narcissism is the voice within that says, "I am the smartest one. I'm the one with the answers. You can come to me for any solutions you need." It's the attitude that convinces you that you're right—all of the time. When narcissism moves into your heart and mind, you love yourself more than you revere the responsibilities of leadership that have been given to you.

Several challenges arise when we begin to examine how to weed out this deadly love of self. The first challenge is that a narcissist, by nature, has a hard time seeing his or her own pride. People around them can't always put their finger on it, either. Maybe they sense something, but don't have the agency to confront the leader. When this dynamic continues for too long, an unhealthy organizational culture results.

THINK OF YOURSELF—BUT NOT THAT HIGHLY. RESPECT YOUR OPINION—BUT NOT OVER OTHERS'.

Here is a challenge, and the key to avoiding narcissism: think of yourself—but not that highly. Respect your opinion—but not over others'. Honor what has happened in life without dishonoring others. Learn what you are learning without minimizing the people in the room beside you. When you can do that, you'll have your pride in check, and you'll be stewarding your leadership well.

Take careful inventory of yourself. A narcissistic leader will always fall.

TAKEAWAY

Think about the legend of Narcissus. Where are you in the story? Are you noticing yourself for the first time? Are you obsessed with your own accomplishments and qualities? Have you toppled into the water and begun to drown? Prayerfully ask God to help you guard your heart against a deadly love of self; commit to whatever He tells you to do.

_____
_____
_____
_____
_____
_____
_____
_____
_____
_____
_____
_____
_____
_____
_____
_____

day 12

LACK OF SELF-AWARENESS

A S LEADERS, IT'S EASY for us to be all too aware of the frantic pace of the world around us. We see our organization, our product, our finances, and our team. We also see everything outside of ourselves. However, it's extremely difficult for most leaders to maintain a regular habit of remaining *self*-aware. In all the chaos and activity going on day to day, we don't pay much attention to what's going on inside of us.

Why is this? Simply put, it's difficult work. Being self-aware requires us to ask the sticky, existential questions: "Why am I here? What's my purpose? Who am I? If I weren't here, what would be different? What will my legacy be?" These aren't five-second answers. Being aware of yourself also includes facing the parts of you that you may not love: self-doubts, fears, challenges, and so many other things.

IN THE DISCOMFORT OF SELF-AWARENESS IS A PRICELESS HIDDEN TREASURE.

Many times, we trade healthy self-awareness for trying to do more, be more, or accomplish more. If we stop to tune into ourselves, we know, we'll realize our capacity has been exhausted. We really haven't been considering our families; we haven't truly taken care of ourselves; we haven't been fully aware of the world surrounding us, even though we think we have.

It seems easier to be overtaken with busyness—to be aware of everything except you. Be careful. In the discomfort of self-awareness is a priceless hidden treasure. Self-awareness keeps you motivated, strong, healthy, and constantly growing. Be the best leader you can be by staying self-aware every day. You'll truly stand out among other leaders, and inspire them to do the same.

TAKEAWAY

What percentage of your day do you spend on yourself—developing yourself, being self-aware? What can you do to increase this percentage, and what will that require giving up in return?

_____

_____

_____

_____

_____

_____

_____

_____

_____

_____

_____

_____

_____

_____

_____

_____

day 13

INTEGRITY AND CHARACTER

NTEGRITY AND CHARACTER. That's all you truly have. At the end of the day, others can take your money, your house, your car—everything you have. But no one can take your integrity and character away from you. It's something only you can give away.

What is integrity? It comes from the Latin word "integer," which means "whole." A totally complete individual is known as somebody with integrity. The two hemispheres to your wholeness are your talk and your walk. These two things have to match. If we have integrity, therefore, there's total congruence between who we are and what we do. When you meet a person with integrity, you know you can trust them. You know their word is good for something. You know they are dependable.

What is character? It's made up of your decisions. Character is something we choose every day, every hour, and every minute. It's purposing that, if nobody ever finds out about your choices, you'll still make the same ones. It's not about who's watching; rather, it's about what's right. Character decisions will find you out sooner or later. If you make choices you're proud of, they'll affect the trajectory of your life. If you make choices you're not proud of, the same thing is true. We can recover from most competency decisions, but a bad character decision can have life-long consequences.

WE CAN RECOVER FROM MOST COMPETENCY DECISIONS, BUT A BAD CHARACTER DECISION CAN HAVE LIFE-LONG CONSEQUENCES.

When your life is whole, and when you have character, you don't have to remember what you said to whom, and keep track of the story—the truth is always the same. That is more precious than anything. You cannot buy character. You cannot buy integrity. They come freely. But, boy, are they expensive!

TAKEAWAY

When you consider character and integrity, which would you say you have developed more at this point in your life? Explain your answer. How are the two intertwined? What can you do to develop your weaker trait this week?

_____

_____

_____

_____

_____

_____

_____

_____

_____

_____

_____

_____

_____

_____

_____

_____

_____

_____

_____

day 14

ASSUME NOTHING

WE ALL HAVE ASSUMPTIONS. If you hear the word "car," or "house," a mental picture immediately pops up. We all do this naturally, and each of our mental pictures will be at least slightly different. Some people might picture a black Lexus; others might conjure up a red, beat-up truck.

Leaders get into trouble by making important decisions based off of assumptions. They assume that others' perspectives, and even their own past methods, will conform to their own mindsets. However, just because something was true last week doesn't necessarily mean it's true today. And just because a leader understands a concept doesn't mean that those he's trying to convey it to will see it the same way. We have to realize that things change, and people are all different in how they think and what they think about!

Leaders must clarify everything and assume nothing. Picture this mindset as a hat that you put on—a non-assumptive hat. Instead of saying, "I know this," your posture says, "I can assume nothing." This hat keeps you on the road of concrete knowledge.

VERIFYING THINGS, AS A LEADER, PUTS YOU IN A PLACE TO KNOW FOR CERTAIN, AND THEREFORE TO MAKE STRONG DECISIONS.

People assume things because they exaggerate their own self-knowledge. However, verifying things, as a leader, puts you in a place to know for certain, and therefore to make strong decisions. Stop assuming. Start digging. Make sure you truly know what you are dealing with. Then, make decisions accordingly.

TAKEAWAY

What assumptions have you been making in your leadership? What different perspectives have you neglected to see in those on your team? How can you accommodate these differences and communicate more effectively?

_____

_____

_____

_____

_____

_____

_____

_____

_____

_____

_____

_____

_____

_____

_____

_____

_____

_____

PART II:
PRODUCTIVITY

day 15

HOW TO UTILIZE CONNECTION AND CONTENT

AS A LEADERSHIP consultant, I get to speak on platforms all over the world. I've spoken in New Zealand, Australia, Brazil, South Africa, India, Nigeria, Ghana, and many other amazing locations! I've also bombed on many platforms. I went into these particular speaking engagements with great content; however, I knew within the first two or three minutes of my talk that it was dead. Why? There was no connection between my audience and me.

Have you ever been there before? Have you felt that sensation, when everything you're sharing is falling flat? After all, you've likely spent hours—days—preparing your content. Why isn't there a connection?

To answer that question, let's take a look at the link between connection and content. If connection is the bridge, and content is the product you need to get across it, which do you think needs to be established first? This is a mistake that many speakers and leaders make. You can't begin with the content. Instead, you must begin by building a connection with your audience!

FOR THE FIRST SIXTY SECONDS OF ANY TALK THAT I GIVE, I OBSESS WITH BUILDING BRIDGES.

For the first sixty seconds of any talk that I give, I obsess with building bridges. My audience members may know me, or they may have never heard of me before. In every case, I have to build that bridge in order to get my content across.

So what are you doing to get your product across? How are you connecting to your audience, your potential clients, your community? I'm here to tell you—from experience—that if you don't connect, you can have the best content, but it won't make your desired impact. Obsess with content; but obsess more with connection.

TAKEAWAY

Which do you tend to focus more on when you address audiences—content or connection? Explain why a speaker needs to excel in both to reach his or her audience.

---

day 16

THE NEED FOR CONSTANT IMPROVEMENT

HAVE YOU EVER heard a world-class athlete or musical prodigy say, "You know what? I'm at the top. I'm a champion. I don't need to improve anymore. I think I'll stop practicing." Of course not! No successful athlete or musician thinks this way.

So why is it that, in leadership circles, we become comfortable doing things how we've always done them? Why don't we engage with constant improvement and development opportunities? The world isn't static—it's always shifting and changing! If you go into cruise control as a leader, what's going to happen is that people will begin to pass you by.

When you reach this point, you're going to try to control others, to lead them out of your own insecurities. If anyone has attempted this before, you can probably attest to the fact that it doesn't work well.

Here's a sentence to say to yourself on a daily basis: "What is it about me that will keep me from becoming the best me that God intended for me to be?"

"WHAT IS IT ABOUT ME THAT WILL KEEP ME FROM BECOMING THE BEST ME THAT GOD INTENDED FOR ME TO BE?"

The only person standing between you and your next level is you. It doesn't matter how good you are right now, in this moment. You have to improve constantly. Begin by not believing what *they* say. Most of us have at least a few people who sing our praises, who flatter us. The moment you begin believing those expressions of admiration—the second you start thinking you're *all that and a bag of chips*—you'll stop improving.

Make a commitment to continually improve. It might be reading, listening, attending a conference, writing, or simply stretching beyond your comfort zone. If you don't improve constantly, you'll hold your organization back. Simply put, you can grow, should grow, and must grow.

TAKEAWAY

What two or three things can you improve on this week? How do you think each of these things will affect your team and your organization?

_____

_____

_____

_____

_____

_____

_____

_____

_____

_____

_____

_____

_____

_____

_____

_____

_____

_____

_____

THE NEED FOR COACHES AND MENTORS

PERHAPS ONE OF the greatest regrets we can have is looking back and realizing we did not have coaches and mentors guiding us. It may seem like a luxury to have someone imparting wisdom into your life; but in leadership, coaches and mentors make all the difference.

Think about athletes. There are tennis and golf stars who are great on their own; but any expert will tell you that they'll never make it to the championships—to the greatest levels of their skill—without someone to guide and train them. There's nobody in our world who's achieving great things without coaches and mentors.

So, why is it that we, as leaders, think we can go forward in the role that the Lord has placed us in without these people?

We see the same principle in God's Word. Timothy and Titus had a Paul. Paul had Aquila and Priscilla and Barnabus. As you read the Scriptures, people have always had mentors in their life. It's part of God's design that we grow together.

THE BEST THING YOU CAN DO FOR YOURSELF IS SURROUND YOURSELF WITH A TEAM WHOSE EXPERIENCE AND WISDOM TAKE YOU TO THE NEXT LEVEL.

You want to go higher. You want to achieve the next level that God has for you. To do that, you need a coach. You need a mentor. Who has permission to speak into your life in a formal, authoritative way? The best thing you can do for yourself is surround yourself with a team whose experience and wisdom take you to the next level. Today, make a list of people you want to approach, and plan to spend time getting to know them.

TAKEAWAY

Make two lists—one list of all the mentors and coaches you currently have in your life, and another list of people you can seek out to be a mentor or coach. What does each person bring to the table that could help you go to the next level?

_____

_____

_____

_____

_____

_____

_____

_____

_____

_____

_____

_____

_____

_____

_____

_____

_____

EVENTS AND PROCESSES

LL ORGANIZATIONS HAVE events and processes. Some organizations say, "We're really good at doing events." Some say, "We're really good at processes." In fact, there's some debate as to which is of greater value. A growing organization— an effective organization—doesn't only hone one of these aspects of their operation; they pay close attention to both.

There's a cycle that exists in planning: events lead to processes lead to events. The real question, then, isn't how great your event is, but rather what your plan is for the process *after* the event. Spend just as much time thinking about what happens around events as you do with the event itself! Most organizations—especially churches—neglect process. However, it's essential to dedicate effort to process in order to maximize your events.

YOUR IMPACT WILL BE SO MUCH GREATER WHEN YOU PAY ATTENTION TO PROCESS.

How you structure your team around these two elements will look different for every organization. The event team may not be the same as the process planning team. Process thinkers are, after all, different in nature from event thinkers. You can have two teams that work in conjunction. Use your intuition, and your knowledge of how your team operates, to find the best method for you.

The bottom line is that your impact will be much greater when you pay attention to process. You'll have momentum to get where you're going and the impact to make a difference along the way.

TAKEAWAY

Do you tend to focus more on events or processes? Why do you think this is? How could you begin to structure your team's responsibilities to ensure that both elements are given equal amounts of attention?

_____

_____

_____

_____

_____

_____

_____

_____

_____

_____

_____

_____

_____

_____

_____

_____

_____

_____

day 19

HOW TO GET THINGS DONE

L EADERS IN EVERY country and industry struggle to get things done. It's no secret that productivity is one of the top subjects of podcasts, books, and other leadership materials today. Leading a team to execute initiatives is challenging at best. Here are three words that will radically improve your team's efficiency:

Who?

What?

When?

Let's put those together into a transformative sentence: "Who does what by when?"

This statement may seem obvious, but it's actually a profound tool that can change the productivity of your meetings. First, you must assign an individual "who" to every task. Otherwise, a task becomes everyone's task, and it never gets done. The point person you designate needs to be your contact for that task—a reliable individual who can follow through. Make sure you choose the right "who."

You must also designate a "what." These are the specific elements of the project. These must be clearly explained at the outset to your "who," or else you'll end up cleaning up the miscommunication at the other end. Be sure to clearly identify what you want.

"WHO DOES WHAT BY WHEN?" THIS SENTENCE HOLDS THE POTENTIAL TO SHIFT THE WAY YOUR TEAM EXECUTES INITIATIVES.

Lastly, you must establish a "when." This is the deadline. Without a deadline, the "what" won't happen. Rather than defaulting to "as soon as possible"—a vague requirement that means different things to different people—lay down a time and date. Once you hold people accountable to the "when," you'll see things get done more quickly than ever.

"Who does what by when?" This sentence holds the potential to shift the way your team executes initiatives. Give it a try this week!

TAKEAWAY

Who, what, and when: which of these three are you excelling at? Which do you need to work on? How can you practically include all three elements in your team meetings from now on?

_____

_____

_____

_____

_____

_____

_____

_____

_____

_____

_____

_____

_____

_____

_____

_____

_____

_____

CLOSING THE LOOP

AS A LEADER, you have a million questions running through your head throughout the day. They may come to you in the shower, or while you're driving home: *Did this project get done? Did that email go out? When is he going to get back to me?"* These things occupy your mind, and understandably so! Leaders around the world suffer from lack of margin. The problem isn't that we're asking these questions. The problem is that, if not controlled and addressed, these questions create angst and take up our creativity and vision. You'll find yourself stressed at the dinner table, not able to be present with those outside of the office.

How do we fix this problem? By closing the loop. In this strategy, the person with an assignment understands that they need to be in regular communication with you, as the leader, about their progress. Organizations rarely, if ever, emphasize good communication enough. When the person responsible closes the loop of communication, he or she enables you to take that project off your mental list because you know how it's progressing.

ORGANIZATIONS IN BOTH SACRED AND SECULAR CIRCLES RARELY, IF EVER, EMPHASIZE GOOD COMMUNICATION ENOUGH.

Now, this sounds great, but I'm about to make it even sweeter. Closing the loop can radically change how you operate and think. Ideally, this update, from this person, will happen before you even have to think or ask about it! If you've trained your team to operate in a "closing the loop" mindset, it will become a part of their everyday routines. You'll see them do it not only with you as the leader, but with one another, as well!

If you're tired of asking for progress updates, and carrying the burdens of those nagging questions out of the office with you, train your team to close the loop with you on assignments. They must understand the need to update you *before* you have to ask. When you don't have to ask, and they take the initiative to give you the information, you'll know this strategy is working for you.

TAKEAWAY

Why do you think organizations, in general, don't emphasize the need for excellent communication? What toll does this take on employees? What about leaders? In your own words, explain how closing the loop could change this dynamic.

_____

_____

_____

_____

_____

_____

_____

_____

_____

_____

_____

_____

_____

_____

_____

_____

_____

_____

day 21

APPLY PRINCIPLES FIRST

T HE MAJORITY OF leaders take steps to better themselves on a regular basis: we go to conferences; we read books; we listen to podcasts and surf Twitter, Instagram, LinkedIn, and Facebook. We are constantly learning new principles every day. We may be tempted to believe that this is enough—the constant flow of information and wisdom, and our exposure to people who share principles to help us become better.

However, just because we learn something doesn't mean we can automatically teach it to others. Many people teach material they haven't yet made their own. They share principles that they haven't yet applied to their own lives. Often, we haven't lived out, chewed on, and made personal the wisdom that we share with our teams.

PRINCIPLES WITHOUT APPLICATION ARE MERELY THEORETICAL KNOWLEDGE.

It's essential that leaders see the implications of the principles we teach—the consequential thinking that follows. Once we connect these dots in our own, personal environments, we can transfer this wisdom to someone else's environment. But if we don't fully grasp the weight of what we learn from those books, conferences, and podcasts, we won't be able to effectively pass it on to others.

Principles without personal application are merely theoretical knowledge. But once you make something your own, you have power behind those principles. In short, don't be in a rush to go out there with the best, newest, biggest toy and teach others. First, make it your own.

TAKEAWAY

Think about a piece of wisdom you've gleaned from a book, conference, podcast, or other source, but haven't yet applied in your own life. How can you go about practicing this principle this week?

_____

_____

_____

_____

_____

_____

_____

_____

_____

_____

_____

_____

_____

_____

_____

_____

_____

_____

PART III:
LEADERSHIP

day 22

HOW TO DEAL WITH CONFLICT

I T DOESN'T MATTER who you are—everybody experiences conflict. In every relationship in our lives, we'll deal with tension and dissension at some point. Conflict is normal, natural, and neutral.

But what exactly is conflict? Why does it come about? To make the most of conflict, we must understand the root of it. Conflict, essentially, is about expectation and reality. The greater the distance between these two things in any relationship, the greater the conflict. This means that, to realize a certain reality in our bonds with others, we first have to create the correct expectation.

In most conflict resolution cases, we simply deal with the reality—what actually happened—rather than asking ourselves what the expectations were on both sides. While expectations may be clear in the mind of the communicator, they may not have been received with clarity by the recipient. This is true on both sides of a conflict. Each party has specific expectations that need to be communicated and respected.

WHENEVER YOU HAVE CONFLICT, STOP, REWIND THE TAPE, AND ASK YOURSELF, "WAS MY EXPECTATION CLEAR?"

In short, conflict resolution is about creating better expectations. When we let others know our expectations, and honor theirs, we set ourselves up to experience a reality that meets the needs of everyone involved.

Last, it's important to note that we want to keep conflict resolution centered on what happened, not *who* or *why*. If you get personal, you're only going to escalate the conflict itself.

Whenever you have conflict, stop, rewind the tape, and ask yourself, "Was my expectation clear?"

TAKEAWAY

Recall a situation in which you didn't clearly communicate your expectations before conflict arose. How could you have changed the outcome by making your expectations clear?

_____

_____

_____

_____

_____

_____

_____

_____

_____

_____

_____

_____

_____

_____

_____

day 23

A LEADER'S BIGGEST RESPONSIBILITY

A LEADER WALKS INTO any room carrying a number of "suitcases." There is a suitcase called "Integrity." There is a suitcase called "Experience." There is a suitcase called "Competency." These suitcases are all different ways of saying, "This is what I bring with me as a leader."

I want to suggest that, as a leader, the biggest suitcase you carry into any room is the suitcase called "Responsibility." Leadership is not about titles. Leadership is not about all the bells and whistles that go with them. Leadership is not about perks and positions. Rather, leadership is about accepting greater amounts of responsibility.

So, what keeps people from getting to a higher level of leadership? The answer is their inability to accept higher levels of responsibility. Leadership has privileges, but those privileges come with a weighty obligation. A leader's responsibilities include being a good role model, training others, keeping a good attitude, saying, "I will go first," volunteering for things outside your purview, being on time, rising with courageous, faith-filled affirmation, holding up your primary leader's arms, and giving your best.

EVERY DAY THAT YOU SHOW UP AS A LEADER YOU BRING A HIGHER LEVEL OF RESPONSIBILITY.

Every day that you show up as a leader you bring a higher level of responsibility. And guess what happens? Whatever you sow, you'll reap. When you are faithful in responsibility, more is given to you; and more responsibility equates to a higher level of leadership. Do you want to go higher as a leader? Take your responsibility level to the next level, and your leadership will go with it. Responsibility equals leadership.

TAKEAWAY

As a leader, what is one thing you need to take more responsibility for this week? What are the practical steps you can take to do so?

_____

_____

_____

_____

_____

_____

_____

_____

_____

_____

_____

_____

_____

_____

_____

_____

_____

_____

day 24

VOLUNTEERS VS. RECRUITS

LEADERS, HAVE YOU ever found that, when you ask for volunteers, the wrong people usually volunteer? These are eager people who can't greet, or smile, but volunteer to be greeters and ushers. People who can't sing want to be on the praise team. People who hate kids want to be in the nursery. Can you relate to this?

And then, you face a bigger problem: how do you un-volunteer a volunteer? You feel stuck. The truth is, your A-level people will usually not volunteer. Your B- and C-level people volunteer; but your A-level people, who are ready to engage, will only join if you ask them to do so: namely, if they are recruited.

What's the difference between a volunteer and a recruit? Volunteers say, "Yeah, I'll help out here!"

Recruits say, "You want me? I'll be there." Two different things attract two different categories of people. If you ask people to go to your website or a kiosk to sign up, A-level people usually won't be the ones to do so. They're waiting to be asked. They're waiting for a relationship to be built.

JESUS NEVER ASKED FOR VOLUNTEERS; HE ALWAYS RECRUITED.

Generational differences also factor in. Boomers are okay with a lifetime commitment. Millennials are just as committed, but for shorter periods of time. The way that you ask—"We need help in youth for the next four months"—makes a huge difference depending on the age group you're trying to recruit.

The best people in your church are waiting to be recruited. Do you know who these individuals are? Do you have a recruiting strategy? Once you've recruited them, do you have a care and development strategy? And finally, do your recruits know that what they're doing is making an eternal difference?

Jesus never asked for volunteers; He always recruited.

TAKEAWAY

Who are your A-level people? How can you adjust your recruiting practices to ensure that you see, communicate with, and effectively invite them into your ministry?

_____

_____

_____

_____

_____

_____

_____

_____

_____

_____

_____

_____

_____

_____

_____

_____

_____

_____

_____

HIGH-IMPACT, HIGH-RISK POSITIONS

WHENEVER I GO INTO an office or church, I see people in the lobby; I see people in the parking lot: employees, volunteers, people who are assigned to these areas. These are what I call high-impact/high-risk people. For instance, the person working in the parking lot is high-impact/high-risk. How they treat visitors coming into the organization holds a lot of weight for the organization.

As an executive, you're placing a lot of risk on these employees: the usher; the greeter; the receptionist. You'll find that your lowest-paid people have the highest impact—hence, they also have the highest risk.

I am astonished that more leaders haven't connected the dots here. They aren't cognizant of the fact that those representing them—those who make the first impression—are a big risk. Often, they fail to evaluate whether this risk is paying off in the long run.

YOUR LOWEST-PAID PEOPLE HAVE THE HIGHEST IMPACT—HENCE, THEY ALSO HAVE THE HIGHEST RISK.

I see people in parking lots with lousy attitudes. I see ushers and greeters who don't know how to usher or greet. I go to customer care counters, and there is no customer care. I see people on the front line, who hold their company's brand in their hand more than anyone else, squandering their opportunity.

Today, I want to challenge you to take an inventory of the people who are high-impact in your organization—the level of risk you're taking with them, and if it's commensurate to the payoff. If a high-impact person isn't worth the risk, then you need to make some hard decisions. Otherwise, your high impact will go in a negative direction.

TAKEAWAY

Are your high-risk team members work the risk? Are they making a good first impression? How can you tell?

_____

_____

_____

_____

_____

_____

_____

_____

_____

_____

_____

_____

_____

_____

_____

_____

_____

_____

THE PRICE OF LEADERSHIP

NELSON MANDELA SPENT 27 years on Robben Island, off the coast of South Africa. He performed hard labor, was beaten, and had no basic human privileges. Mandela's future appeared bleak. But then, one day, he gained his freedom. One day, he walked out of that prison to change the world.

As leaders, we must remember that leadership comes with a price. Some of you may even be going through that season of refinement right now. Maybe your passion is to change the world, but you're facing massive difficulties. Maybe you have no idea how God's calling in your life will come to be. Maybe you're in your Robben Island prison right now.

Just like Nelson Mandela, keep waiting and preparing—during the fifth year, the fifteenth year, the twenty-fifth year. Despite how you feel, know that a brighter future is coming. God is using this season to prepare you. The Nelson Mandela we celebrate today would not have been the same man without Robben Island. The work you'll do for the Lord requires that you allow Him to shape, mold, and refine you beforehand. That is the price of leadership.

THE NELSON MANDELA WE CELEBRATE TODAY WOULD NOT HAVE BEEN THE SAME MAN WITHOUT ROBBEN ISLAND.

And one day...it will all be worth it. Say to yourself today, "I'm a world-changer. I won't give up. This is my calling. And it's going to be awesome." Don't give up. Stay right where you are, and get ready to move to a brand new place at the right time.

TAKEAWAY

Have you ever been in a season or situation that feels like prison? How does Nelson Mandela's story give you a new perspective of these seasons of trial and waiting?

_____

_____

_____

_____

_____

_____

_____

_____

_____

_____

_____

_____

_____

_____

_____

_____

_____

_____

day 27

THE PRIVILEGE OF SENIORITY

MANY OF YOU are senior leaders right now. Many of you are going to become senior leaders. I want to share a few things with you, regardless of where in your career you happen to be, about the privilege of seniority.

Senior leaders have longevity. This means that they have a responsibility, a need, to mentor others. Your task is not simply to fulfill your responsibilities or to give orders; rather, your calling is to take people on a journey. The privilege of seniority is that you get to bring others up through some of the same lessons, channels, and experiences that you walked through. Remember your mentors and those who supported you? Now, it's your turn.

Another key truth about senior leaders is that they must remain humble. Never let seniority equate to competence in your mind. When somebody says, "I have twenty-five years' experience," you don't know for sure that they truly grew that entire time. They may simply have repeated their first year of experience 25 times. You can't expect longevity to be equal to leadership competency. So, again, we must remain humble as senior leaders.

YOUR TASK IS NOT SIMPLY TO FULFILL YOUR RESPONSIBILITIES OR TO GIVE ORDERS; RATHER, YOUR CALLING IS TO TAKE PEOPLE ON A JOURNEY.

Lastly, we've got to keep changing our minds. What you thought about something last year might not be relevant or accurate today, because information keeps changing. I'm not talking about right, wrong, sin, and the absolutes; I'm talking about how you lead an organization. Be willing to change your mind! That's a lost art in today's society.

Trust the leaders coming up under you. Somewhere, somebody trusted you. So don't hoard your equity and responsibility: always trust others. As a senior leader, also make sure you add equity to *your* supervisor. Always be for him or her. Simply said, seniority comes with privileges—make the most of them.

TAKEAWAY

Think about the individuals you lead on a daily basis. How can you show these people that you trust them, and take them on a journey? Think about your senior leader. How can you better help them succeed?

_____

_____

_____

_____

_____

_____

_____

_____

_____

_____

_____

_____

_____

_____

_____

_____

_____

day 28

THE PURPOSE OF AN ORGANIZATIONAL STRUCTURE

N 2016, I stayed with wonderful hosts in Ghana, West Africa, on a trip. My hosts placed me in a gorgeous residence filled with villas—I even got my own, personal villa! This Ghana trip caused me to reflect on the purpose of organizational structures, and their roles in getting us to our destinations. Allow me to explain.

The purpose of an organizational structure is to help you fulfill the mission—the vision—of your organization. Whether you work in a church or a corporation, structure helps you achieve your goal. It's similar in function to the cars, trains, and planes that helped me get to Ghana. Each of these vehicles played a part; but alone, none of them could do the job. My goal was not the car, the train, or the plane—my goal was to get to my destination.

THAT'S WHAT HAPPENS WHEN YOU BEGIN WITH AN ORGANIZATIONAL STRUCTURE INSTEAD OF A VISION—YOU LIMIT YOUR DESTINATION!

So if I had insisted, "I only want a plane to get me there," I would never have seen my villa. That's what happens when you begin with an organizational structure instead of a vision—you limit your destination! However, once you have a destination in mind, then you can decide, "What kind of organizational structure will allow me to get there?"

As a consultant, I hear this question all the time: "Dr. Chand, what is the best structure for our church or corporation?" I'm here to tell you that this is the wrong question. The right question is "What's our destination? What do we want to achieve?" Once you know that, you can decide the structure that will help you get there.

Don't put the cart before the horse; let the horse lead the cart. Happy traveling!

TAKEAWAY

Before you can decide on the organizational structure you need, it's essential to have a clear vision of where you're going. Below, outline your vision in detail—what does it look like? How will you know when you've arrived?

_____

_____

_____

_____

_____

_____

_____

_____

_____

_____

_____

_____

_____

_____

_____

_____

_____

day 29

OVERTRAINED AND UNDERDEVELOPED

EVELOPMENT AND TRAINING are two totally different things. Most organizations are over-trained and underdeveloped. What's the difference? I'm glad you asked.

Training is about a task—what you do. Development is about a person. It's about understanding the impact and the outcome of your work. Many people are trained, but never developed by their leadership. Training simply tells you, "This is what you do." But development tells us why we are there in the first place!

Now, how does development happen? It happens when we invest time in people. Development is what I call the soft side of leadership. Training is the hard side of leadership. Training is easy; development is difficult, because it calls for mentoring and coaching.

All of us know people who can deliver on a job given to them; however, in the process, they run over people. They kill people. They're rude to people. And then you, as a leader, have to go behind them trying to clean up the mess they created.

TRAINING SIMPLY TELLS YOU, "THIS IS WHAT YOU DO." BUT DEVELOPMENT TELLS US WHY WE ARE THERE IN THE FIRST PLACE!

Do you know why this happens? Because these team members are overtrained and underdeveloped. However, when you get a good person—someone you can trust—someone who is a good example of who you are—now you have somebody developed *and* trained. It's not "either/or." It's "both/and." You need to make sure that your people are developed as well as trained.

TAKEAWAY

Why do you think most leaders don't take the necessary measures to develop their staffs? How do you think you can reframe development for your team, so that you and your fellow leaders get excited about developing those underneath you?

_____

_____

_____

_____

_____

_____

_____

_____

_____

_____

_____

_____

_____

_____

_____

_____

FUNCTIONAL VS. ORGANIZATIONAL LEADERS

THINK ABOUT THE transitions that brought you to where you are today. In my experience, there are two phases that all leaders go through in their experience. We begin in one place, and move into another form of leadership as we mature. Let me share with you these two phases of leadership.

Everybody starts off as a functional leader. If their trajectory takes them in the right direction, they end up being organizational leaders. We begin by functioning on projects—we are put charge of things. When you do this well enough, somebody eventually comes by and says, "You know what? He's a good functional leader; maybe he can be an organizational leader as well. Maybe he can lead people." This transition sounds simple, but this is where the biggest leadership challenges lie.

THERE HAVE BEEN MANY EXCEPTIONALLY GOOD FUNCTIONAL LEADERS RUINED BECAUSE SOMEBODY THOUGHT THEY'D MAKE GOOD ORGANIZATIONAL LEADERS.

When somebody moves from being a functional leader to an organizational leader, they make a major shift. After all, *things* don't talk back to you; people do. *Things* don't have separate opinions, attitudes, and wills; people do. This is an entirely different hemisphere, and the transition here is the biggest challenge most leaders will ever face.

Whenever you move somebody from being a functional leader to an organizational leader, think hard and long about it. How are they with people? How do they manage conflict? Are they self-disciplined? Are they self-starters? Are they people who understand communication? Are they people who really get it?

Many exceptionally functional leaders have been ruined because somebody thought they'd make good organizational leaders. Just because someone thrives in one hemisphere doesn't mean they will thrive in the other.

TAKEAWAY

What practical steps do you think are important to take when transitioning someone from being a functional leader to an organizational leader? If someone doesn't adapt well to these steps, might it be better to leave them in a functional leadership role?

_____

_____

_____

_____

_____

_____

_____

_____

_____

_____

_____

_____

_____

_____

_____

day 31

3 THINGS TO KNOW ABOUT STAFFING

STAFFING ISN'T AS simple as, "How do we get people into the right slots?" There's an art, a science, to it. We need three key elements in our hiring process.

Need. Many times, people choose to hire because there was previously a position in the organization that they now want to fill. The problem with this strategy is that there must also be a legitimate need for a paid staff member. Think about it: if you can get a volunteer to fill a role, you may not have to pay someone.

So, start by saying, "Do we have a need? Is it a legitimate need? Is it yesterday's need, or tomorrow's need?

Who can fill this need? Can a recruited volunteer do the job as well as a paid staff member?"

START WITH A NEED; CREATE A PREFERRED PROFILE; AND HUMANIZE YOUR ONBOARDING PROCESS.

Preferred Profile. You've got to know what kind of person is going to meet your need in the best way. A preferred profile may include demographics, experience, education, availability, and other factors. By setting these criteria, you ensure your interviewees have the ability to meet them (or not). In organizations today, hiring teams tend to start with a person—which is the worst place to start. Starting with a person keeps you from starting with the need and truly assessing who you need in that role.

Onboarding Process. This goes beyond HR's policies and procedures; this is about bringing people into your culture—helping them understand your DNA. You've got to introduce new hires to the team and get their feet wet in a genuine, connected way. If you don't onboard in the right manner, the longevity, morale, competency, and expectation of your team will be skewed.

In short, start with a need; create a preferred profile; and humanize your onboarding process. These steps will set you up for a truly effective staffing process.

TAKEAWAY

In your organization's current hiring process, do you tend to start by looking at a person or looking at your need? Explain your answer.

_____

_____

_____

_____

_____

_____

_____

_____

_____

_____

_____

_____

_____

_____

_____

_____

_____

day 32

WHAT YOU CAN NEVER DELEGATE

D ELEGATION IS A word frequently tossed around in organizational circles. Delegation is deciding who can help us do something. There's a difference between dumping and delegating: dumping is when you pass off something you simply don't want to do. You probably know how it feels to be on the other end of that. Delegation, in contrast, is respectfully yielding in trust to someone who can do the job better than you.

We tend to glorify delegation as the key to successful organizations. While it's healthy and needed, there are certain leadership responsibilities you simply cannot delegate. For instance, the senior pastor of a church can't delegate vision-casting. He must set the vision and tone for the organization. He also can't delegate the executive tasks and decisions he has to make each day. These are all things for which he's responsible because of his role.

WHEN EVERYONE IS CLEAR ABOUT WHAT THEY SHOULD AND SHOULDN'T PASS OFF TO SOMEONE ELSE, THERE WILL BE LESS CONFUSION, FRUSTRATION, RESENTMENT, AND CONFLICT AMONG TEAM MEMBERS.

Even if you're not an executive leader, you have tasks and responsibilities that fall under your purview. There are certain things you can't delegate. Recognizing this won't just benefit you; it will also benefit your relationships with your co-workers. When everyone is clear about what they should and shouldn't pass off to someone else, there will be less confusion, frustration, resentment, and conflict among team members.

The list of what you can delegate is long—and it should be listed somewhere. However, you also must make a list of those critical responsibilities that you can't delegate. Take ownership of those things. Commit to seeing them through. Make that list right now. What is it that you can never delegate in your leadership role?

TAKEAWAY

Think about your position and its responsibilities. What duties and tasks are uniquely yours? What responsibilities cannot be passed on to someone else?

_____

_____

_____

_____

_____

_____

_____

_____

_____

_____

_____

_____

_____

_____

_____

_____

_____

_____

_____

day 33

SEGMENT YOUR LEADERSHIP

WHAT MADE JESUS the most successful leader that's ever walked the earth? Well, there are many answers to that question. One important answer is that Jesus understood that segmentation of leadership is very important.

Think about the structure He built into His leadership—His relationship with others. Jesus had the crowd, the 70, the 12, and the 3. All four of these groups had different functions. The three disciples helped Him think. The twelve disciples helped Him organize. The seventy disciples helped Him do. The crowd was for public relations. Why did Jesus take the 3 to the most intimate times in His life? Because they were at a different level than the rest of His followers.

Our challenge, as leaders, is that we tend to think everyone is equal. While it's true that everyone's equal in God's sight, we also know from the Parable of the Talents that different people have different capacities and giftings.

JESUS HAD THE CROWD, THE 70, THE 12, AND THE 3. ALL FOUR OF THESE GROUPS HAD DIFFERENT FUNCTIONS.

If you give your thinking people things to organize, they will have a hard time. If you give your thinking people things to do, nothing will get done. Everyone on your team has different abilities and callings. Once you understand that, you'll be able to segment those you lead, just as Jesus did, into appropriate spaces and responsibilities.

When this happens, you create margin for people to develop and grow from where they are: a doer can progress to being an organizer; an organizer can end up developing into a thinker.

It's not about the numbers in each category; it's about understanding that the people on your team are not equal. Never treat people equally; do, however, treat them fairly. The capacities and giftings of those under you are most evidenced when you know that you have to segment your leadership.

TAKEAWAY

Jesus had four main groups of followers, each with specific responsibilities and giftings. How many groups of people do you have under your leadership? Make lists of who is in each group and what characteristics each group shares.

_____
_____
_____
_____
_____
_____
_____
_____
_____
_____
_____
_____
_____
_____
_____
_____
_____
_____

day 34

LEADING INTO THE UNKNOWN

PERHAPS YOU'VE HEARD the saying, "You cannot take people where you haven't gone yourself." This seems logical; however, I have found that this saying isn't true. Every major leader, whether they lead in spiritual, political, or social circles, has led people to places they have never been themselves. In fact, leadership requires this! Let me explain.

Think about some of the most prominent leaders in our society. The odds are that they haven't had experience in their role for a long period of time. It may even be that their role requires them to take on new, foreign responsibilities, and lead into new places. The president of any country has never been president before his term. The pastor of a megachurch hasn't been a pastor for his entire lifetime. A life-saving doctor has to train and practice, working his way up to his first official day.

THE HIGHEST LEVEL OF LEADERSHIP IS BEING ABLE TO LEAD IN AMBIGUITY. AFTER ALL, HOW YOU LEAD PEOPLE WHEN YOU'RE UNCERTAIN REVEALS YOUR LEADERSHIP SKILLS.

Leadership is all about walking into new territory. No true leader leads people only to places they've already been; rather, they lead into the new. In this kind of environment, certainty fades away, leaving uncertainty.

The highest level of leadership is being able to lead in ambiguity. After all, how you lead people when you're uncertain reveals your leadership skills: your thinking, your way of motivating others, your inner sustainability, your willingness to look at your options, and your willingness to gather a team around you.

All these things come into play when you realize you are taking people where you yourself have never been. So, what new territory are you venturing into today? Who are you taking with you?

TAKEAWAY

In your leadership sphere, what is the foreign, unknown territory that you're leading people into currently? Whether you lead a business, church, nonprofit, or home, you are treading unfamiliar ground—and that's a good thing!

_____

_____

_____

_____

_____

_____

_____

_____

_____

_____

_____

_____

_____

_____

_____

_____

day 35

TAKING STAFF FOR GRANTED

ONE OF THE greatest challenges for leaders today is communicating appreciation to their team members. It's easy for time and energy to slip through our fingers. There are a multitude of responsibilities on our shoulders, and those under our leadership have their own duties, as well. As the days slip by, it can become extremely easy for us to begin taking our teams for granted.

Whether you have a paid team or a team of volunteers, this is a struggle you'll face at some point. Complacency and forgetfulness can result in our teams not feeling as appreciated as we want them to feel. When this happens, we must remember one key thing: our success, our future, and all the possibilities ahead are not contingent on us. They're contingent on our team!

No one is a one-man success. It takes a team to achieve great things. This is why it's your ladder-holders that determine how successful you will be. If they are equipped, prepared, and appreciated, they will take you higher. If they are taken for granted, neglected, and unappreciated, they will burn out and take you with them.

YOU CAN MAKE ALL THE GREAT PRODUCT AND IMPRESSIVE STRIDES IN THE WORLD; HOWEVER, YOUR TEAM WILL BE THE ONES WHO PULL IT ALL TOGETHER.

Leaders, remember this going into your week: you can make all the great product and impressive strides in the world; however, your team will be the ones who pull it all together. Your team will be the people to present and champion your vision to the world. They are the ones with skin in the game, as well, and they are real people with real feelings and thoughts.

You can't take any of them for granted. People are smart. They can sense when they're being honored, included, respected. They can also sense when you forget about them, fail to acknowledge them, and don't care about their lives. Nobody wants to be taken for granted—not even you!

TAKEAWAY

Think about the people on your team and their unique gifts, contributions, and likes. Brainstorm a handful of ways that you can express your appreciation to them this week—be as specific as possible.

_____

_____

_____

_____

_____

_____

_____

_____

_____

_____

_____

_____

_____

_____

_____

_____

_____

_____

day 36

EXPLOITING THOSE WHO TRUST YOU

HAVE YOU EVER been betrayed by someone you trusted? It stings, doesn't it? Not only did they lie to you, but, for whatever period of time they did so, they knowingly exploited your faith in them. You may wonder, "How long has this been going on? You acted like everything was fine between us!"

These instances are a painful reminder that we must never exploit anyone's trust. How do you ensure you never do this? The consequences of exploitation aren't limited to you, or even to your inner circle. The higher you go, the more your decisions affect everyone underneath you.

Your personal decisions are more consequential than your professional decisions. Think about it: if you make a poor professional decision, what happens? You lose money, momentum, business connections, or a bit of reputation. If you make a poor personal decision...? You've seen them plastered all over the news. You're going to lose the only real currency you have: trust. Your legacy, and the legacies of those connected to you, could be destroyed.

BE SURE THAT YOUR PERSONAL AND PROFESSIONAL LIVES MATCH ONE ANOTHER. THAT'S HOW YOU CAN ENSURE THAT YOUR LEGACY IS PROTECTED.

So understand the weight of your decisions. Never exploit someone else's trust. Be sure that your personal and professional lives match one another. That's how you can ensure that your legacy is protected.

TAKEAWAY

Think about the personal and professional repercussions of breaking someone else's trust. Can you think of anyone in your life, or in the news, who exploited someone and suffered a hard fall because of it?

_____

_____

_____

_____

_____

_____

_____

_____

_____

_____

_____

_____

_____

_____

_____

_____

_____

day 37

HOW TO RETAIN LEADERS LONG-TERM

WE ALL WANT to retain our leaders for the long haul. Regardless of what others suggest, it's not money, title, position, or other incentives you can offer them. You retain leaders long-term by genuinely being interested in them as people. This seems like a simplistic solution, but consider it with me for a moment. What's the number one key to team member satisfaction? It's not a paycheck, though that may be up there. It's a healthy work environment. If someone doesn't feel appreciated—doesn't feel you are interested in them—they're not likely to stick around, no matter how much other incentive is present.

On the flip side, as long as your leaders know that you are genuinely interested in them (not only what they do, though that is important, as well), they will follow you anywhere. You'll find that taking genuine interest in your leaders helps you retain them more effectively than anything else.

YOU'LL FIND THAT TAKING GENUINE INTEREST IN YOUR LEADERS HELPS YOU RETAIN THEM MORE EFFECTIVELY THAN ANYTHING ELSE.

Historically, the best generals, political figures, and other leaders displayed this wisdom: they built teams of people willing to give up their very lives. Why were their teams this loyal? It wasn't simply because of the cause they fought for, but because they knew their leader believed in them and had actual, personal interest in them.

Here's a question for the leaders: How do you demonstrate genuine, personal interest in your team? Here's the reason you must do so: Every turnover in your organization costs you market share, leadership equity, onboarding costs, time, energy, money, and resources. You see, it's in your interest to retain leaders. And you do that in one way: being personally interested in them as human beings.

TAKEAWAY

In what practical ways do you take interest in your leaders? What will it cost you not to do so?

_____

_____

_____

_____

_____

_____

_____

_____

_____

_____

_____

_____

_____

_____

_____

_____

_____

_____

_____

_____

_____

THREATENED BY EMERGING LEADERS

A HUGE CHALLENGE, in corporate and church circles, is the dissonance between incoming, emerging leaders, and present, established leaders.

Established leaders, if they are not careful, start playing not to lose, rather than playing to win. They grow defensive of their positions and leadership equity; they grow jealous of incoming leaders, not wanting to share with or invest in them. They see shortcomings in these emerging individuals, who seem to climb much too quickly compared to their own laborious journey into leadership.

Emerging leaders, on the other hand, are playing to win. They are excited, passionate, and eager to climb. They don't have years of failures in their memories, and they don't believe that achieving a higher level of leadership should necessarily take decades.

YOU MUST PREPARE THE ESTABLISHED LEADERS FOR THE EMERGING LEADERS. PREPARE THE CRUCIBLE—THE VESSEL—THE ORGANIZATION—SO YOU CAN PUT NEW LEADERS INTO IT.

This dichotomy creates two different mindsets—two different value systems. One of the greatest challenges *lead* leaders face is this tension. If you're leading an organization and you're not having this challenge, you probably have a pretty complacent organization. It means you don't have any leadership percolating or in the works.

Once you recognize that this tension exists, you must prepare the established leaders for the emerging leaders. Prepare the crucible—the vessel—the organization—so you can put new leaders into it. Hone in on your existing leaders, bring them up to speed, prepare them with open arms; and you'll find that they respect, honor, and receive your emerging leaders.

TAKEAWAY

How can you show your established leaders that you see and appreciate their years of work and heart? At the same time, how can you implement practices that encourage and validate emerging leaders?

_____
_____
_____
_____
_____
_____
_____
_____
_____
_____
_____
_____
_____
_____
_____
_____
_____
_____

PART IV:
CULTURE

day 39

DON'T DO YOUR OWN THING

AS A TRAVELING speaker, I get to visit all kinds of environments and cultures. Each invitation I've received is from an individual with a special passion and unique vision for his or her event. Here are a few tips on how to conduct yourself when you're invited to speak somewhere outside of your usual environment.

Whether you have a date on the calendar, are thinking about speaking somewhere, or simply praying about where God wants you to go next, it's essential to serve the agenda of the person who invited you. When you journey to an event or organization that isn't yours, there will inevitably be a new mission, or vision, separate from your own. That event was created for a purpose. You were invited for a purpose—that's a great honor! Now, you need to be sure that you bring your personal agenda in line with your inviter's agenda.

ONCE YOU MAKE UP YOUR MIND THAT IT'S NOT ABOUT YOU, YOU'LL REALIZE THAT YOUR GREATEST ANOINTING, WHILE YOU'RE ABROAD SPEAKING, IS TO HELP THOSE WHO INVITED YOU SUCCEED.

After all, they did not invite you to do your thing, but to do their thing. Spiritually, you must bring yourself under their covering. Simply put, do what they want you to do. Stay within the parameters they set—whether it's time limits, topics, or any other requirements.

It goes back to the idea of holding someone's ladder. Each leader has people who are holding their ladder. As a traveling speaker, you are called to help hold the ladder of those leading the event or organization. Once you make up your mind that it's not about you, you'll realize that your greatest anointing, while you're abroad speaking, is to help those who invited you succeed. Do that, and they'll be sure to invite you back.

TAKEAWAY

If you guest speak in any capacity, consider some questions you can ask those who invite you. How can you clarify their vision so that you're sure to champion it during your time at their event?

_____

_____

_____

_____

_____

_____

_____

_____

_____

_____

_____

_____

_____

_____

_____

_____

_____

_____

_____

day 40

THIS IS HOW WE DO THINGS HERE

EVERY PLACE HAS a culture. Your home has a culture. Your workplace has a culture. The restaurant you frequent has a culture. A bus station has a culture. Every city has a culture. Every nation has a culture.

I want to talk to you about the culture of your organization. Can I define culture for you? Very simply put, culture says, "This is how we do things here." That's all it is.

In my book, *Cracking Your Church's Culture Code,* I take the word "culture" and make an acronym out of it. I'd like to share that acronym with you now. Pay attention to each element of culture—they're all essential.

C: Control. Who's really in control of your organization?

U: Understanding. Does everyone know why you exist? What's the "why" behind your "what?"

L: Leadership. How do leaders get promoted, developed, and deployed in your organization?

T: Trust. This is in the center because it's the most important. Everything moves at the speed of trust.

U: Unafraid. When you have a culture with no fear, you will have authenticity, transparency, and creativity.

R: Responsive. Is your culture a place where people keep in touch? Do they get responses?

E: Execution. Are things actually getting done?

EVERY PLACE HAS A CULTURE. YOUR HOME HAS A CULTURE. YOUR WORKPLACE HAS A CULTURE. THE RESTAURANT YOU FREQUENT HAS A CULTURE.

What is the culture of your house? Culture is stronger than vision. Many people focus on vision and not culture. However, in my book, I make this point: "A toxic culture will eat vision for lunch."

TAKEAWAY

Which letter of the CULTURE acronym do you have down pretty well? Which letter do you most need to work on in your organization?

_____

_____

_____

_____

_____

_____

_____

_____

_____

_____

_____

_____

_____

_____

_____

_____

_____

_____

_____

_____

THE PRIMACY OF RELATIONSHIPS

AVE YOU EVER stopped and asked yourself, "How did I get here?"

You might answer: "Well, because I went to college, studied for this subject, got a diploma, submitted an application, and went through the process." However, I'd like to submit to you that those answers don't explain how you got anywhere.

There's only one reason why you are doing what you're doing today: relationships.

You and I are a product of serial relationships. One person introduced you to the next person, who introduced you to the next person—and you carry all those relationships with you. So, if we know that we're a product of all the people who have brought us to where we are, why do we become so busy that we don't invest in relationships?

GENUINE, AUTHENTIC, TRANSPARENT, TRUSTING RELATIONSHIPS ARE WHAT BROUGHT YOU HERE, AND THEY WILL TAKE YOU TO WHERE YOU WANT TO GO.

Relationships are sitting around you in the room right now. Here's a question for you: what are you doing to increase your relationship equity? Who are the people with whom you need to be in communication? Your competency can be great, but relationships will get your competency noticed by somebody else.

Commit to making a list of people you can reach out to this year. Increase your relationship equity. Be intentional to cultivate it. Add value to somebody else. Genuine, authentic, transparent, trusting relationships are what brought you here, and they will take you to where you want to go.

TAKEAWAY

Is there anyone you need to thank for their help in getting you to where you are today? Make a list of these people. Make a second list of people in your world that you'd like to reach out to this year.

_____

_____

_____

_____

_____

_____

_____

_____

_____

_____

_____

_____

_____

_____

_____

_____

_____

_____

day 42

THE IMPORTANCE OF ALIGNMENT

THERE ARE THREE things you must align before you can move forward in your organization. Before we explore these three things, let's examine what misalignment does to your organization.

Have you ever driven a car that had a wheel out of alignment? You have to fight to keep the car on the road or to make sure you're not going to run into the car next to you. Your hands shake; your shoulders hurt. You've got four wheels; only one is out of alignment; but still, you're having to work amazingly hard just to keep the car on the road. This is how important alignment is in your organization.

The first thing you have to align in your organization is the people. Unless you get the "who" right, the "what" is irrelevant. In my book, *Who's Holding Your Ladder?* I talk about the primacy of getting the right people. When Jesus was on this planet, the number one thing He did was get the right people on His team. People alignment is integral to where you are going. You can't choose just anybody. It's better to have a vacancy than bad help, because a vacancy may not hurt you; bad help will.

YOU'VE GOT TO MAKE SURE YOUR PEOPLE, PURPOSE, AND PROCESS ARE ALL ALIGNED.

The second thing you must align is your purpose. Your purpose is your "why." Unless people are aligned with their "why," they will never be able to give the energy you expect.

And finally, you must align your process—this is your "how." The same process doesn't work every time, in every situation. You've got to make sure your people, purpose, and process are all aligned. Unless the "how" is done right, every step forward will become laborious and slow for your organization.

When all three of these things are in alignment, your car will drive easily, and your leadership role will be that much more manageable.

TAKEAWAY

Reflect briefly below on the alignment of your people, purpose, and process. Are the wheels on your car working together to move you forward? How can you improve your alignment?

_____

_____

_____

_____

_____

_____

_____

_____

_____

_____

_____

_____

_____

_____

_____

_____

_____

_____

_____

day 43

4 TYPES OF PEOPLE

D O YOU HAVE a person on your team who consistently doesn't deliver? Do you have ongoing frustration because of team members who don't meet expectations?

When you go through this struggle, this principle will free you: we have to understand that not all people have the same gifts, talents, competencies, and wavelengths. There are four main types of people in an organization. Let's look at each one.

Wanderers. These people will never truly "get it." You can invest in them all day long, show them videos, invite them to conferences, etc. It won't make a difference. These can be good people who know the Lord, but they simply don't have the ability to catch the wave of your organization.

Followers. These people see it, but they won't pursue it on their own. You can tell them to straighten chairs or clean rooms, and they will. However, they don't take the initiative to do things; they don't pursue the vision of their own accord.

Achievers. These people see and pursue the vision. They go after it. This is where we tend to get satisfied: when a team member can deliver. However, there's a key difference between achievers and leaders.

LEADERS DO THREE THINGS WELL: THEY SEE THE VISION, THEY PURSUE IT, AND THEY HELP OTHERS SEE IT.

Leaders. Leaders do three things well: they see the vision, they pursue it, and—here's the difference—they help others see it. They know, they grow, and they show.

Once we understand these four categories, we can meet people where they are, for what they can contribute at any given time. This will free you from a lot of heartache and frustration and improve your relationships with those around you.

TAKEAWAY

Consider the people in your organization. Have you misidentified any of them as a leader when they're actually a wanderer? What about vice versa? How can misidentifying your team members lead to frustration for both you and them?

_____

_____

_____

_____

_____

_____

_____

_____

_____

_____

_____

_____

_____

_____

_____

_____

_____

_____

PLAYING NOT TO LOSE

WHAT'S THE DIFFERENCE between a team who's playing to win, and a team who's playing not to lose?

First, here's an obvious fact: if you're playing not to lose, you're ahead in the score. You're winning. That's when teams get complacent, right? They start playing defense, protecting what's supposedly already theirs. However, we've seen too many sports matches end in surprise twists and leave teams that were playing not to lose disappointed and in shock.

Playing not to lose takes away your appetite for risk; your innovation; your fearlessness. You settle, not venturing into places you've never been, because what's worked in the past seems to be adequate for the present.

Teams who are playing to win, however, are not looking simply at the score. They're actually playing to win against themselves—against the team they were during the last game. They are constantly taking risks, constantly improving, and constantly innovating. Teams like this respect and honor everyone's role in the effort—even those in the stands. Teams that are playing to win know that winning isn't an accomplishment sought after for oneself, but that, when you go up, you always take others with you.

PLAYING NOT TO LOSE TAKES AWAY YOUR APPETITE FOR RISK; YOUR INNOVATION; YOUR FEARLESSNESS.

So, here's an exploratory question for you: is your organization playing to win? Or have you started, slowly but surely, playing not to lose?

TAKEAWAY

What would change in your organization if you shifted your focus from the "score" to improving yourself as a whole? How might such a shift in perspective affect your definition of "winning?"

_____

_____

_____

_____

_____

_____

_____

_____

_____

_____

_____

_____

_____

_____

_____

_____

_____

_____

_____

day 45

RESTORING YOUR LUSTER

T HE TAJ MAHAL in India is one of the seven wonders of the world. However, there's something happening underneath (or rather, on) the surface of the Taj Mahal that everyone knows about. The luster—the shine—of the marble is eroding because of the pollution in the air. Chemicals, smog, and toxicity have taken their toll over hundreds of years.

To see the Taj Mahal today is to behold a gorgeous feat of architecture and a rich symbol of history; and yet, it's not the same as it once was. By the time two or three more generations have grown up, it may not look the same as it does today.

Did you know that this same erosion happens to organizations? Think about the original luster that you began with—the vision you had at the start. You started by building wonderful things: structures, people, churches. But, after a while, the culture, disappointments, exits and entrances, all started to remove the shine of your organization. Real life happened. The honeymoon phase ended. Now, you may still see a beautiful organization, but you know that it looks different than it once did.

THINK ABOUT YOUR ORGANIZATION. WHAT WILL IT TAKE TO GET THAT LUSTER—THAT SPARKLE AND FIZZ—BACK AGAIN?

We don't like to recognize this reality; but recognizing it is essential to reversing the process. Those who care for the Taj Mahal have stopped and said, "What do we need to do to regain our luster?" It should be no surprise when we must do the same.

Think about your organization. What will it take to get that luster—that sparkle and fizz—back again? What will it take to make it look the way you've always seen it in your mind? It's all about restoring, and preserving, your luster."

TAKEAWAY

Recall your organization or venture when it first began. What excited you? What did the dawn of your enterprise look like? What do you need to do to recover that initial luster?

_____

_____

_____

_____

_____

_____

_____

_____

_____

_____

_____

_____

_____

_____

_____

_____

_____

_____

day 46

POWER VS. AUTHORITY

HAVE YOU EVER thought about what differentiates power and authority, and how one comes to possess them?

The difference between the two lies in their definitions. Power is bred from a title or position; someone who has power over you can intimidate you, or hold you to certain standards. They can require things of you. They can even dismiss you, if they choose. The power someone has comes from the position they hold over you.

Authority, on the other hand, is not position-driven. It doesn't come with a title or salary. Authority is earned. To gain authority, someone must demonstrate value and wisdom to those around them. Unlike power, authority has to be granted from others.

You can obtain and display authority in many different ways: you can have authority on a certain subject matter; authority in the way you conduct yourself; authority through your attitude; authority through how you respect others; authority in how you help others; authority by how you invest in other people who are not part of your trajectory; and an endless array of other ways.

UNLIKE POWER, AUTHORITY HAS TO BE GRANTED FROM OTHERS.

In short, power is inherited, but authority is earned. Authority comes from other people seeing value in you, and authorizing you to lead them.

What can you do today to invest in others so that they trust you with authority over them? How can you make the leap from power to authority?

TAKEAWAY

How do you think today's culture has affected the way we view power and authority? Which do you think is more important to have as a leader? Explain your answer.

_____

_____

_____

_____

_____

_____

_____

_____

_____

_____

_____

_____

_____

_____

_____

_____

_____

_____

A TIME AND PLACE FOR TRANSPARENCY

THERE ARE DIFFERENT levels of transparency when it comes to our relationships with others. Some people are barely transparent. These people share little personal information, preferring to keep their lives private and out of the public spotlight.

Other individuals fall along the middle of the spectrum: they'll divulge personal stories and information, but they know the difference between what's personal and what's confidential. These people know when to share, and when to stay silent.

A third group of people lay everything on the line. These are the people who post every detail and woe of their days on social media. They monopolize your time, giving you nitty-gritty details about their problems (details you probably didn't care to know). They allow all their stories and faults into the public eye.

WHENEVER YOU'RE PREPARING TO BE TRANSPARENT AS A LEADER, ASK YOURSELF THIS QUESTION: "WHAT IS THE PURPOSE OF MY BEING TRANSPARENT IN THIS SITUATION?"

Where you fall along the transparency spectrum depends upon your purpose in being transparent. Transparency for its own sake isn't necessarily healthy. However, if you're a leader being transparent for the purpose of organizational growth, you can leverage this to benefit those around you.

Whenever you're preparing to be transparent as a leader, ask yourself this question: "What is the purpose of my being transparent in this situation?" Once you determine your purpose, you can use transparency to bring transformation.

TAKEAWAY

What might some good reasons be for transparency in your organization? What are some unhealthy reasons people tend to be transparent?

_____

_____

_____

_____

_____

_____

_____

_____

_____

_____

_____

_____

_____

_____

_____

_____

_____

_____

_____

day 48

GIVING AND RECEIVING FEEDBACK

EVERYBODY WANTS FEEDBACK, right? Well... maybe not. It depends on the kind of feedback we're talking about. After all, most people love positive feedback. If you have good feedback for me, yay! But if it's constructive or instructional in nature, something defensive in us usually resists that.

We tend to see it as a one-time conversation, but feedback is a process. Whether we're giving or receiving it, we need to know how to navigate that process. Let's take a look at a few quick principles about feedback.

When you're giving feedback to someone else, it's imperative that you do it respectfully (that is, if you hope to get your point across). Don't expect the recipient, in those first moments, to respond to you with total acceptance. People will usually respond by thanking you. At the same time, they may be thinking something completely ungrateful. After all, this is the first they've heard of the issue. Operate with understanding and respect, leaving your feedback without a demanding spirit.

FEEDBACK IS NOT A ONE-TIME CONVERSATION; IT'S AN ONGOING DIALOGUE.

When you're on the other end of the feedback, respect is also paramount. You must understand that other person's observations have value, as well. They make a difference just as much as you do. Value feedback, and say to the person providing it, "Thank you. Give me some time to think about that."

Feedback is not a one-time conversation; it's an ongoing dialogue. Make sure your part in that dialogue is courteous, constructive, and life-giving. Chances are, when it's your turn to be on the receiving end, people will give you the same courtesy.

TAKEAWAY

Do you tend to struggle more with giving or receiving feedback? Why do you think this is?

_____

_____

_____

_____

_____

_____

_____

_____

_____

_____

_____

_____

_____

_____

_____

_____

_____

_____

_____

_____

day 49

WHY YOUR TEAM FEELS INADEQUATE

A S LEADERS, THERE are subtle, often unseen, ways in which we make our teams feel inadequate. Let's explore just a few.

Your team feels inadequate when you're always the hero of the story—when it's always about you. You'll know you're slipping into this when every story, every success, is attributable to your contribution. Obviously, that makes the other team members involved feel inadequate.

Another way we make others feel inferior is by communicating that what they do is never good enough. When we never praise them, never give positive feedback, and never tell them that they are needed and wanted, our teams quickly become discouraged. In fact, they may become convinced that they're unable to perform their responsibilities!

IF YOUR TEAM NEVER FEELS INADEQUATE, THEY WILL BE ABLE TO REACH FOR HIGHER THINGS—AND TAKE YOU WITH THEM.

A third way we make our team members feel inadequate is when we give them tasks above their competency, *without* acknowledging that up front. If we take the time to tell them, "I'm going to stretch you with this assignment, because I believe in you," that takes away the feelings of inadequacy from the task.

Finally, beware of backhanded compliments. You may have been the subject of one of these in the past. Backhanded compliments involve thanking somebody, but passive-aggressively making a cutting remark at the same time. This takes all the celebration out of the conversation, and hurts the person on the receiving end of your "feedback."

If they never feel adequate, your team will crumble in insecurity and discouragement. If, however, your team never feels inadequate, they will be able to reach for higher things—and take you with them.

TAKEAWAY

Why do you think many leaders fall into the trap of belittling their teams? What do you think is at the root of this desire to make others feel inferior? How can you guard against this temptation in your own leadership?

_____

_____

_____

_____

_____

_____

_____

_____

_____

_____

_____

_____

_____

_____

_____

_____

_____

day 50

ADDRESSING INTERNAL CONFLICT

HAVE YOU EVER walked into a meeting and sensed conflict in the room? We like to camouflage it—disguise it in jokes and passive-aggressive behaviors; but still, it's relatively easy to see when internal conflicts are happening in your organization.

The air in the room changes during conflict. Things are tense. People don't talk openly to one another. Hurt feelings seem to radiate, and productivity plummets. Though it's relatively easy to feel this tension in the room, solving it is much more complicated.

What's astounding is that many lead leaders see and recognize this, yet never take the next step: they never do anything to resolve the conflict. Leaders see two of their employees who have ongoing, continual conflict—and everyone else sees it too. However, they carry on with business as usual, and don't address it. When this happens, the culture of the room—and even, in extreme cases, the team—becomes toxic and unhealthy.

UNLESS YOU HAVE THE COURAGE AND FORTITUDE TO CALL CONFLICT OUT WHEN YOU SEE IT, IT WILL SIMMER AND BOIL OVER, AFFECTING YOUR ENTIRE ORGANIZATION.

As a leader, one of your primary responsibilities is to handle conflicts within your team. If those under you can't trust you as a reliable mediator, you'll only be able to watch helplessly as tensions take over your culture.

Unless you have the courage and fortitude to call conflict out when you see it, it will simmer and boil over, affecting your entire organization. Your direction won't be good; your destination will be even worse. If you're a lead leader or team member, know this: your internal conflicts will derail you faster than any external challenge. To function well as an organization, you must be healthy on the inside. Only then can you turn and successfully face the challenges coming at you from the outside.

TAKEAWAY

Have you ever had a leader who effectively addressed and dealt with team conflict? If so, describe what he or she did that stood out to you. How do you think you can go about practically dealing with conflicts, either presently or in the future?

_____

_____

_____

_____

_____

_____

_____

_____

_____

_____

_____

_____

_____

_____

_____

_____

_____

_____

day 51

LEARNING FROM SUCCESS

HOW DO WE learn from success? It begins by changing the way we debrief. Say your team has just put on an event. Afterwards, everyone who was involved gets together to debrief and review how things went. It's likely that the conversation will center around what went wrong. People will ask, "How can we improve? What could we do better?"

This can be constructive up to a point—then it simply becomes discouraging. What's better is to spend the majority of the time obsessing about what your team was successful at doing. What went right? What happened that was good? What do you want to repeat? Once you find your successes, you discover exactly what you are going to repeat and leverage again in the future.

When you focus on the positives, your team will walk away from the debriefing knowing that they effectively contributed to a good endeavor. In addition, wins will seem even more possible in the future, because you've affirmed and celebrated the wins they just accomplished.

THE MOST IMPORTANT QUESTION YOU CAN ASK IS, "WHERE DID WE SHINE? AND HOW CAN WE MAKE THAT HAPPEN AGAIN?"

So, the main question your team should be asking around the debrief table is not, "Where did we fail?" The most important question you ask is, "Where did we shine? And how can we make that happen again?"

Obsess with what is right, and you will go higher in life. Focus on the victories, and your team will go to the next level.

TAKEAWAY

What are some practical ways to ensure that your debriefings are balanced between positive celebration and constructive feedback?

_____

_____

_____

_____

_____

_____

_____

_____

_____

_____

_____

_____

_____

_____

_____

_____

_____

_____

IMPLEMENTING YOUR DECISIONS

AS LEADERS, WE often see decisions as complete once they've been made. However, there's another aspect to decisions that plays out only after we've made a call. While decision-making takes place in contained environments—behind conference room doors, over the phone, or in a video call—decision implementation affects your entire organization.

For instance, take the decision to hire—or fire—an employee. Yes, that decision is made by the leadership team, but it has consequences for everyone else. That person who is brought on, or let go, will touch everyone, even if the decision was made by a minority of the staff. If they're joining the team, everyone will need to get to know them and learn how to work with them; if they are leaving, there are adjustments to be made in emotional terms and in assigned responsibilities.

DON'T ASSUME THAT, BECAUSE DECISIONS HAVE BEEN MADE, THE IMPLEMENTATION PROCESS WILL BE AUTOMATICALLY SMOOTH.

Many leaders focus solely on making decisions, and try to let the details of how they're carried out fall onto others' shoulders. But this lack of an implementation strategy can be disastrous. Don't assume that, because decisions have been made, the implementation process will be automatically smooth. Instead, spend more time developing an implementation strategy. In the long run, it will actually save you time and energy.

Your decisions are great, and you've likely thought them through. Now, to ensure that those decisions are lasting, develop an implementation strategy. The one is never complete without the other.

TAKEAWAY

Are you intimidated by the process of implementing your decisions? Why or why not? What do you think your team members—those under your leadership—need to succeed as you implement your decisions?

ABOUT THE AUTHOR

D R. SAM CHAND is a leadership architect and consultant, author, change strategist, speaker, and dream releaser whose life vision is helping others succeed. From businesses to ministries, Dr. Chand helps leaders find their vision, create healthy cultures, and empower their teams to achieve their goals. Chand has also created a wealth of leadership resources, including the Sam Chand Leadership Institute and Tuesdays with Sam Chand, a weekly video series designed to encourage and inspire both leaders and teams. Dr. Chand and his family live in Atlanta, Georgia.

CPSIA information can be obtained
at www.ICGtesting.com
Printed in the USA
FSHW011358060420

9 781950 718214